GHOSTS OF THE WEST COAST

GHOSTS OF THE WEST COAST

The Lost Souls of the Queen Mary

and Other Real-Life Hauntings

TED WOOD

WALKER AND COMPANY

NEW YORK

To the memory of my grandparents, who taught me the power of fact and mystery

First published in the United States of America in 1999 by Walker Publishing Company, Inc.

Published simultaneously in Canada by Fitzhenry & Whiteside, Markham, Ontario L3R 4T8

Library of Congress Cataloging-in-Publication Data
Wood, Ted.
     Ghosts of the west coast: the lost souls of the
Queen Mary and other real-life hauntings/Ted Wood.
        p. cm. —(Haunted America)
     Includes index.
     Summary: Chronicles true ghost stories from Washington State, Oregon,
and California, including those about the gold miners of Bodie State
Historic Park, the Whaley House in San Diego, and the Heceta Head
Lighthouse.
     ISBN 0-8027-8668-5 (hardcover). —ISBN 0-8027-8669-3 (reinforced)
     1.Ghosts—Pacific Coast (U.S.)—Juvenile literature. [1. Ghosts—Pacific Coast (U.S.)] I. Title. II. Series.
BF1472.U6W664 1999
133.1'09795—dc21
                                          98-26718
                                              CIP
                                              AC

BOOK DESIGN BY DIANE HOBBING OF SNAP-HAUS GRAPHICS

Printed in Hong Kong
10 9 8 7 6 5 4 3 2 1

CONTENTS

Introduction

It was a warm, windless day in San Jose, California, and I had just finished photographing the bedroom of Sarah Winchester, the former owner of the strangest, most-visited ghost mansion in the world—the Winchester Mystery House. I walked outside into the garden, past dozens of families touring the house, and wondered what I was doing there. How could a place that had more tourists than bats and cobwebs possibly have a ghost too?

I looked up to the third-story bedroom I had just left, when one of the windows slowly opened. I watched in disbelief as an unseen hand opened the window all the way, where it

At night, bathed in an eerie light, the Winchester Mystery House seems to come alive with restless spirits.

7

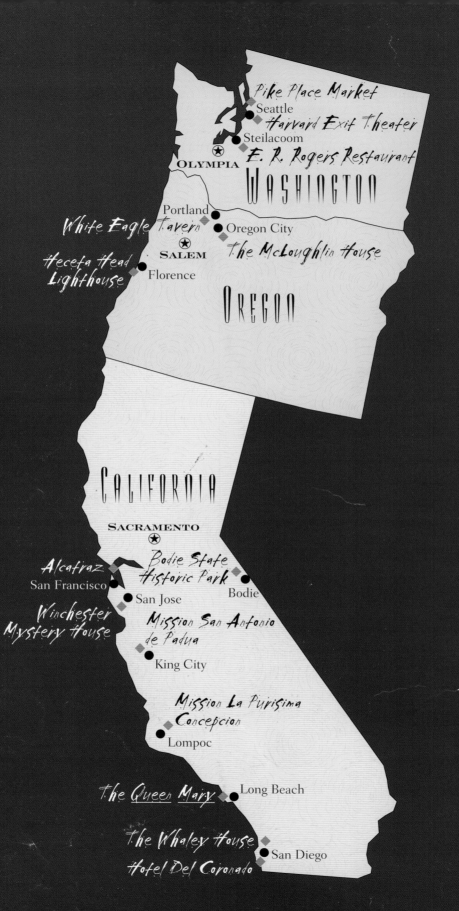

Pike Place Market
Seattle
Harvard Exit Theater
Steilacoom
E. R. Rogers Restaurant
OLYMPIA
WASHINGTON

Portland
Oregon City
White Eagle Tavern
SALEM
The McLoughlin House
Heceta Head Lighthouse
Florence
OREGON

CALIFORNIA

SACRAMENTO

Bodie State Historic Park
Alcatraz
San Francisco
Bodie
San Jose
Winchester Mystery House
Mission San Antonio de Padua
King City

Mission La Purisima Concepcion
Lompoc

The Queen Mary
Long Beach

The Whaley House
San Diego
Hotel Del Coronado

Even toy stores can be haunted, especially the Toys "R" Us in Sunnyvale, California.

stayed until I walked off. Did I just have a ghost encounter? I wondered. In broad daylight, with so many people around?

Though I'll never know for sure, there's no reason why I didn't catch a glimpse of Mrs. Winchester at work. Real ghosts, unlike Hollywood ghosts, don't follow scripts. Encounters are reported during all hours of the day, in shopping malls, restaurants, museums, and even markets.

Would you believe that a Toys "R" Us store could be haunted? I didn't until I visited one in Sunnyvale, California. Workers told me about toys flying off shelves, sounds of horses galloping on the second floor, and cold winds whipping down certain aisles. Kids now come by the store looking for a ghost encounter as much as a new toy.

Some places are supposed to be haunted but aren't. I had heard that Hollywood was crawling with ghosts of movie stars. Marilyn Monroe and some of her pals were said to haunt Hollywood's Roosevelt Hotel—playing trumpets, appearing in mirrors, and making phantom phone calls from empty rooms. It made perfect sense to me that in Hollywood, death would never be the final act for some stars. But these stories turned out to be more movie-town magic. Marilyn and her friends were nowhere to be seen by me or anyone else, except on Hollywood's silver screens.

All of the places in this book, from California to Washington, have a long history of ghost encounters that are still going strong today. The stories come from people who were lucky, or unlucky, enough to bump into the resident spooks. However, I couldn't resist adding some Hollywood magic of my own to the photos. The pictured ghosts are not dead movie stars but very live human beings in ghostly getups.

For the moment, leave behind that scary darkness deep in your basement and the creepy neighborhood house bristling with menace and mysterious shadows. Follow this road map to the unknown side of everyday places. Come explore these haunted sites that everyone can visit but that reveal their secrets only to the brave and curious ghost hunter.

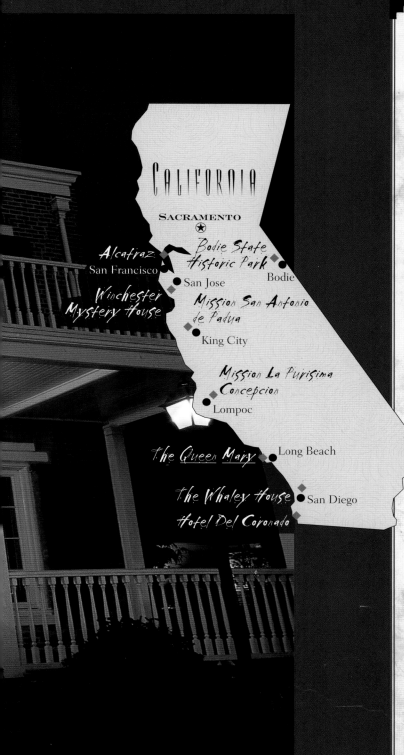

CALIFORNIA
SACRAMENTO ★

Alcatraz
San Francisco

Winchester
Mystery House

Bodie State
Historic Park

San Jose

Bodie

Mission San Antonio
de Padua

King City

Mission La Purisima
Concepcion

Lompoc

The Queen Mary

Long Beach

The Whaley House
Hotel Del Coronado

San Diego

1

CALIFORNIA

The Whaley House, San Diego

HAUNTED BY

Thomas and Anna Whaley, Yankee Jim Robinson, and little Annabelle Washburn

It's called the most haunted house in California. The number of ghosts seen in this small San Diego museum

Ghosts have walked the Whaley House for more than 140 years, and even today new spirits pop up on a regular basis.

1 1

*When Anna Whaley plays her broken piano,
the sound of one eerie chord fills the house.*

grows each year, as if the spirits in the nearby graveyard can't resist a good hair-raising get-together.

Even in 1857, when the house was first built, a ghost already waited for a family to haunt. Unknown to the Whaleys, their new home was built on land once used for hanging criminals. "Yankee Jim" Robinson had been hanged five years earlier for stealing a boat. But instead of a quick death, Yankee Jim suffered for fifteen agonizing minutes, cursing his executioners all the while.

His revenge began as soon as the Whaleys moved in and hasn't stopped since. Gary Beck, who now helps run the museum, hears Jim's phantom footsteps creaking over the doorway to the first-floor music parlor, the room built where the hanging gallows once stood. Sometimes, visitors are overcome by a sudden choking sensation as they stand in the doorway. Could it be the feel of the hangman's noose?

Not to be outdone by Yankee Jim, the ghosts of Thomas and Anna Whaley also remain in their beloved home. After closing time, Gary smells Thomas's cigar smoke, hears papers rustling in his empty office, and sees a shadowy form moving from room to room downstairs. Visitors have seen a man dressed in old-fashioned clothing descending the stairs only to disappear before their eyes.

On a tour upstairs one day, Gary and three visitors watched in amazement as a bluish white form of a woman materialized in a bedroom and began folding imaginary clothes. The ghost, Gary told his terrified guests, was Anna Whaley. Often he smells her phantom cooking coming from the old kitchen, and sees her sitting at her piano where she always plays the same chord, just once, then disappears. The music is especially spooky, Gary says, because the piano hasn't worked for years.

Outside in the garden, people witness a glowing white Anna watering her flowers at dawn, and see the spirit of Annabelle Washburn, a neighborhood child who died after running into the Whaleys' clothesline, playing on the lawn.

In fact, Gary hears so many new accounts from startled visitors and staff—rooms full of disembodied voices, cold spots, even apparitions of long-dead local Indians—that he can't say how many ghosts are gathering at the Whaley House. Or more important, why?

In the early dawn light, Anna Whaley can be seen tending her garden.

Hotel Del Coronado, San Diego

HAUNTED BY

Kate Morgan

It was a slow night in 1997 in the gift shop of the Hotel Del Coronado. Lupita hadn't worked there long and wanted to learn more about San Diego's grand old hotel. She was reading a book about the Del's famous ghost, Kate Morgan, when she felt a hand on her back and cold breath on her neck. Her hair stood straight up, she said, and she slowly turned to see a shadow moving into the clothing corner of the store. Suddenly, hats came flying off the shelves, and Lupita went flying out of the store, wondering if the job was really worth it.

How Kate Morgan became a ghost is as much a mystery as her hotel pranks. In 1892, a young, beautiful Kate checked into the hotel expecting to meet her cardsharp husband, Tom. Kate was pregnant, and Tom had promised to give up his gambling ways for his family-to-be.

But Tom never came. Desperate, Kate purchased a gun and shot herself in the head on the hotel beach. Or did she? What was long considered a suicide changed to murder

The century-old mystery of Kate Morgan's murder lives on at the Hotel Del Coronado, along with her ghost.

Room 3502 is one of two haunted rooms where the spirit of Kate Morgan appears to certain guests.

when it was later discovered that the lethal bullet was not from her gun but from another. Was Tom the murderer? Is Kate's ghost offering clues to her unsolved death? To this day, no one knows.

But one fact is known: Strange things happen in Room 3312, Kate's room. One guest saw a woman's face materialize on his turned-off television and ran to the lobby. Two staff members returned with him and saw the face as it faded away. For years a young boy and his father vacationing at the Del always took Room 3312 because the boy liked to talk to the "beautiful woman in black." Now grown up, the boy no longer comes.

This same woman in black is seen in and around Room 3502. In Kate's day this was the room of a maid who mysteriously disappeared soon after Kate's death. Was she connected to the murder? Many think so because 3502 is much more active than Kate's old room. Ashtrays fly off tables, water faucets turn themselves off and on, the toilet flushes by itself, and the room temperature goes from boiling hot to freezing cold.

Even guests in both rooms who have never heard Kate's story often report an eerie feeling of being watched. Perhaps Kate is looking for just the right person to reveal her secret to—a lucky youngster who might finally hear the true story from the "beautiful woman in black."

The Queen Mary, Long Beach

HAUNTED BY

Crewman John Pedder, World War II sailors, and long-ago passengers

It's not easy getting aboard a ghost ship; one second it's there, the next second it's not. But the *Queen Mary* is as real as the water it floats on. It's the ship's passengers that are the phantoms.

Built in the 1930s to ferry people across the North Atlantic in splendor, this luxury liner made more than one thousand crossings before taking its last great cruise to Long Beach Harbor, where it was permanently anchored

The Queen Mary may be the most haunted ship in the world.

In the ship's hotel, a woman in a white gown floats down the hallways and dances by herself in the first-class lounge.

in 1967 and turned into a hotel. The *Queen Mary* is huge—over three football fields long and twelve stories high. There are miles of spooky hallways and passages inside, where visitors continue to bump into the lost souls prowling the ship.

The ghost of an eighteen-year-old crewman named John Pedder is seen wandering around the engine room where an airtight door crushed him to death during an emergency drill in 1966. For more than thirty years, people have reported seeing the same bearded man dressed in dirty blue overalls disappear as he walks toward the murdering door.

Deep in the ship's bow, another horrifying accident is replayed by the lingering victims. During World War II, the *Queen Mary* collided with the British cruiser *Curaçao*, cutting it in half. The cruiser sank in fifteen minutes, taking 338 sailors to their watery graves. The sound of men crying, moaning, and shrieking has frequently been heard at the collision point. A tape recorder that was left on overnight even picked up eerie banging and scraping on the hull—sounds of a boat breaking apart.

A few decks above, there's a beautiful indoor swimming pool where the first-class passengers took refuge from the bitter North Atlantic weather. Though the pool is no longer used, night watchmen frequently hear splashing sounds and women's voices. When they investigate, there's nothing but wet footprints on the floor. Could it be hotel guests sneaking a swim? Probably not, because the pool is empty! Most likely, it's the two women ghosts that guides and visitors see playing in the pool, both in old-time bathing suits. One ghost even dives into the empty pool, to the horror of unsuspecting onlookers.

There seems to be a ghost everywhere on the *Queen Mary*. The entire middle deck where hotel guests stay is haunted, the staff claims. A beautiful woman in a flowing white gown floats across the lobby and into the Queen's Salon, the old first-class lounge, where she dances alone. One guest was roused from his sleep by the sound of boots stomping in the hall. When he peeked out his door, he witnessed a troop of ghost-sailors marching down the long deck. He checked out that night. Some people, it seems, just get ghost sick.

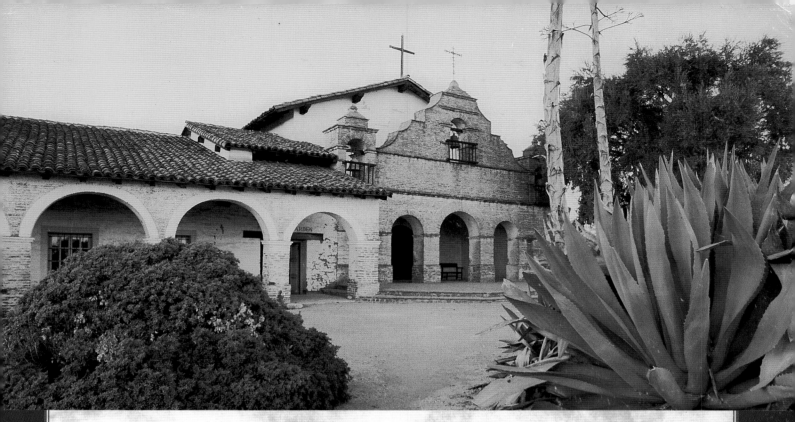

Mission San Antonio de Padua, King City
Mission La Purisima Concepcion, Lompoc

HAUNTED BY

Spanish monks

Among the freeways and subdivisions of Southern California, the old Spanish missions are doorways to another century, where spirits of the past live peacefully within the thick adobe walls.

California's missions are mysterious windows into the past, and some, like Mission San Antonio de Padua, offer ghostly extras.

In Mission San Antonio de Padua, a hooded monk holding a candle floats through the inner courtyard at night.

Mission San Antonio de Padua lies in a forgotten valley near King City, surrounded by Fort Hunter Liggett military base. Ever since the mission was built in 1771 by Spanish monks, there have been reports of paranormal happenings in and around the central courtyard—cold spots, flickering lights, and unseen presences.

It was here in 1978 that the country's best-known ghost hunter, Richard Senate, encountered a monk late one night in the courtyard. The hooded friar was ten feet away from Richard when he suddenly vanished. It was Richard's first ghost sighting.

Farther to the south in Lompoc, Mission La Purisima Concepcion has another spirit friar. Steve Jones has been a ranger in this state historic park for ten years, and recently he met the ghost that's been haunting the mission for decades.

In one of the mission's bedrooms, the old bed still looks the way it did one hundred years ago—a simple wooden frame with a straw mattress and a blanket. But for some unknown reason, the bed will not stay made. Ever since 1941, rangers have been straightening the blanket only to return later and find it wrinkled with an impression in the mattress, as if someone had been sitting down.

On Mischief Night, 1997, the night before Halloween, Steve entered the room to get a wig from the costume closet adjoining the room. There are no lights in the room, so Steve pointed his flashlight at the bed, which he had made up earlier. Not only was the blanket messed up again, but sitting on the mattress was a long-haired man in an old gown. Startled, Steve jumped back into the doorway. His flashlight mysteriously went out. In the dark, scared, he fiddled with the light until the beam again lit up the bed. Now the figure was standing, looking at him.

Instead of feeling fear, Steve felt a sense of peace. The man was smoky white, not quite solid, but very visible. Somehow Steve knew the apparition was friendly. He said hello to the ghost and told him that he was just passing through. The ghost followed Steve to the costume closet, stood behind him as he got the wig, and followed him back to the outside door. The ghost was never more than an arm's length away.

Steve has seen him many times since, always near the same room. From his research, Steve believes the bed phantom is Father Mariano Payeras, the Spanish padre who headed the mission. He died in the bedroom in 1823 and was buried in the chapel under the altar.

Although Steve doesn't know why the padre chooses to appear only to him, he feels honored. But according to Steve, anyone can witness the unmade bed phenomenon. It happens so often that Steve promises you'll leave the mission with a ghost story of your own.

Bodie State Historic Park, Bodie

HAUNTED BY

Gold miners and other rowdy pioneers

"Good-bye God, I'm going to Bodie," wrote a little girl in 1879 as her family left for the wild, remote gold mining town on the Nevada border.

Wild it was with seventy-five saloons, thirty mines, and ten thousand adventurous miners. Killings were a daily event, with all the stickups and drunken street fights. To a young girl, it must have seemed a crazy, upside-down world.

But Bodie's hot temper cooled and died when the gold ran dry. The residents left behind everything when they fled town, including some of their spirits. Today it is a ghost town suspended in the past and preserved as a state park.

The saloon in the Wheaton & Hollis Hotel is still a high-spirited place, where phantom miners are seen drinking beer and playing pool.

When darkness creeps into Bodie and the park visitors leave for the day, a few brave rangers return to the town's old houses where they live year round. Not long ago, a new ranger came to Bodie and moved into the Donnelly House, originally home to the town butcher. He was lonely without his two cats, which he had to leave behind. The first night he dreamed of the cats, how they slept on either side of him like bookends. He woke up once and thought he felt their weight pressing against him.

The next night he didn't dream of cats, but he woke up again feeling the same pressing weight. He thought about the ghost stories he'd heard and wondered if they might be true. The third night he awoke pinned under the covers, as if two people were sitting on either side of him, trapping him under his blankets. But

Bodie was once a wild mining town high in the California desert, but it's now filled only with wind, dust, and plenty of ghosts.

there was nothing on the bed, except for the impressions of two sitting phantoms.

"Stop it," he yelled, more mad than scared. "I know you're here, but please leave me alone." As if it were nothing more than a ghostly welcome, the blankets smoothed out and the weight disappeared, never to bother the ranger again.

Down the street from the Donnelly House is the Wheaton & Hollis Hotel, where visitors have reported seeing a man dressed like a miner drinking a beer at the bar, and hearing the sound of pool balls hitting each other in a ghostly game.

Perhaps the most haunted complex is the Old Fellows Lodge and the Dechambeau Hotel. A woman's ghost is sometimes seen peering out of a second-floor hotel room, while next door in the Lodge, the sound of foot stomping erupts some evenings, as if dozens of men are pounding their feet in a rowdy meeting. Many of the park workers are scared to enter the complex.

But one ranger, who didn't believe these tall tales, bet that he could spend the whole night with the ghosts upstairs in the Dechambeau. When his friends unlocked the door the next morning, the ranger rushed out, pale and shaking. Without a word, he quit his job and left Bodie. The ranger's ghost encounters disappeared with him, but the ghosts didn't. The saloon brawls and gunfights may be long gone, but Bodie's nightlife seems to be as wild as ever.

The Swazey Hotel and other nearby saloons formed the wicked, rowdy center of Bodie in the 1870s. Today the area is home to most of Bodie's ghosts.

Winchester Mystery House, San Jose

HAUNTED BY

Sarah Winchester and victims of her husband's rifles

The Winchester Mystery House in San Jose is not just a ghost house; it's a house designed by ghosts for ghosts.

In 1881, William Winchester, the Winchester rifle heir, died in Connecticut, leaving his fortune to his wife, Sarah. But the money couldn't ease Sarah's fears that a ghostly curse was descending on her. She was sure that evil spirits had taken both her husband and her baby girl who had died fifteen years earlier. Believing that her recently departed husband could help her, Sarah contacted his spirit through a medium.

In its time the Winchester Mystery House was the largest private home in the world. It was built to house the ghosts of those killed by Winchester rifles.

Sarah Winchester spent most of her life terrified of the ghosts in her house. Today, Sarah's ghost does most of the scaring from the bedroom where she died.

"This is a warning," the medium said to Sarah. "You will be haunted forever by the ghosts of those killed by Winchester rifles, unless you make amends to them."

The medium told her to journey west and find a house for all the angry spirits. She must add rooms constantly for all the new victims of Winchester rifles. If she did, the ghosts would let her live peacefully. If not, she would soon die.

Sarah roamed the West for two years, looking for the perfect home. In 1884, she found it, a small house on a big estate in San Jose. She started construction immediately, fearing the ghosts' curse. For thirty-eight years, Sarah added to her wonder house. At night she slipped into the Blue Room, a secret chamber where she received building plans from her spirit guides. Some of those killed by her husband's rifles must have been evil men, Sarah thought, so she tried to design ways to keep their ghosts from getting her.

Sarah believed that the number thirteen could magically keep evil away. She built thirteen bathrooms and forty stairways, each with thirteen steps. Each chandelier has thirteen lights, rooms have thirteen windows, and the windows have thirteen panes.

She slept in a different bedroom every night so the bad ghosts couldn't find her. There are secret passageways, doors that open to blank walls, elevators and stairways that go nowhere, and chimneys that stop before entering the ceiling so ghosts can't sneak in. Every detail was designed to keep Sarah one step ahead of her pursuers. The house became so complex the servants needed a map to find their way around.

Sarah treated the good spirits like royal guests. She prepared lavish banquets in their honor, serving five-course meals on solid gold plates. But Sarah was the only living soul invited. Her long table had twelve dinner settings with Sarah sitting in the thirteenth chair presiding over her invisible phantom guests.

In 1922, Sarah died at age eighty-two, leaving behind a 160-room puzzle house, the largest and weirdest private home in the world. Today, tour guides and workers see her presence in the bedroom where she died and hear piano playing coming from the grand ballroom. As a ghost, Sarah has finally joined the high-spirited party she began over one hundred years ago.

Alcatraz, San Francisco Bay

Convicts

Franco Kelsey has the scariest job on Alcatraz, if not in the country. When the last tour boat leaves the island for San Francisco, and the creeping fog and darkness race to cover the Rock, Franco is left behind, alone in the old prison. Franco

Alcatraz Island, for years America's most infamous prison and now a popular state park, is still home to a few imprisoned ghosts.

is the night watchman on Alcatraz. With no convicts to guard, Franco roams the dark windy walls guarding the prison. There's no one to break out anymore, just nuts who want to break in. But Franco isn't afraid of people. It's the remains of people that bother him.

On Franco's first night on the job, in 1993, he entered the huge cellblock building that once held the prisoners. He walked past the empty cells with his flashlight, listening to the bay wind move through the hallways and steel bars. Suddenly he had that "I'm not alone" feeling and heard a man sneeze behind him. He turned around, thinking he'd caught a trespasser, but no one was there.

Then, in the old kitchen at the end of the hall, he heard an explosion. Franco ran out of the building, shaking. In three years, he's never gotten used to the sounds in the cellhouse. He's heard voices coming from the cells, singing in the hallways, and a harmonica playing taps. Franco doesn't go in there unless he has to. Nor will he go near certain areas—like the shower room, where people have reported being touched on the neck; or the hospital on the second floor, where a disembodied voice once asked a terrified worker, "What the hell are you doing here?" One recent morning, an unsuspecting worker came in earlier than usual to sweep the cellhouse before the prison opened. As he pushed his broom down the hall, he heard chains rattling behind him. He swept faster, but the sound followed him all over the cellblock.

Alcatraz once housed some of the toughest criminals in the country, including Al Capone and Machine Gun Kelly, but no one can say who the imprisoned spirits are. No prisoner ever escaped from Alcatraz and lived to talk about it. Even death, it seems, wasn't a sure ticket off the Rock.

Is it the wind whipping through the cells or the ghosts of former inmates that make the unexplained sounds heard in the prison?

29

OREGON

Heceta Head Lighthouse, Florence

HAUNTED BY

Rue

Along Oregon's rocky, storm-lashed coast, a lighthouse stands high on a cliff, sending out a beam of light so strong that only the curve of the earth eventually hides it from ships.

Like mysterious castles, lighthouses have always had their ghost stories.

The cliffs of Heceta Head hold the spirit of the lightkeeper's wife who forever longs for her baby girl lost to the sea.

White Eagle Tavern
Portland
Oregon City
SALEM
The McLoughlin House
Heceta Head Lighthouse
Florence

OREGON

The lightkeeper's house, now a hotel, may look like a scary place to spend the night, but Rue is a friendly, playful ghost.

But at Heceta Head, it was the caretaker's house farther down the cliff that attracted the ghost.

Old fishermen tell the story of Rue, a lightkeeper's wife who lived in the house in the early 1900s. One day, while Rue was upstairs, her baby daughter toddled out of the house and disappeared. She was never found, but people assumed that she fell over the cliff into the sea. Rue died of old age, but her spirit stayed in the cliff house, forever waiting for her lost child to return.

Today, the lightkeeper's house is a small inn run by Mike and Carol Korgan. They first heard about Rue when the house was being renovated in the early 1970s. A carpenter fixing a broken window in the attic saw an old lady in a gray dress floating across the room toward him. Just a few feet away she vanished. The terrified carpenter packed up and never returned. The next morning the broken glass in the attic had been swept into a neat pile by some phantom broom.

"Rue cares greatly for the house," Carol said. A fresh lavender scent floats through the upstairs guest rooms, but no flowers can be found. Once, a newly-wed couple returned from a walk to find all of their items neatly arranged in their room. Carol hadn't been in the room all week, but apparently Rue couldn't stand the mess.

Another couple, celebrating their twenty-fifth anniversary, had a more personal experience. At 4 A.M. one morning, the woman awoke to a strange electrical buzzing near her head. She was too scared to open her eyes, but she could see a light coming through her eyelids. She raised her hand toward the buzzing and felt a gentle touch. The buzzing then moved away. She opened her eyes and saw a floating ball of red light, like a huge firefly, pass through the door. She thought it was all a dream, until the next morning when her husband asked if she had seen the strange glowing ball over their bed.

Rue's greatest pleasure seems to come from teasing Mike. She moves his slippers while he's asleep at night, hides his hats in the attic, and adds milk to his breakfast oatmeal when he's not looking.

In summertime, Carol and Mike give tours through their haunted inn, telling tales of Rue's antics to those brave enough to listen. Sometimes a sweet lavender smell spreads through the group, and everyone knows Rue is close by, watching.

The McLoughlin House, Oregon City

HAUNTED BY

John and Marguerite McLoughlin

Everything seemed normal at the McLoughlin House until the 1970s, when the remains of John and Marguerite McLoughlin were finally laid to rest next to their old home. Since 1909, the house has been a museum, the oldest in Oregon,

The most haunted room in the house is John McLoughlin's bedroom, where his ghost still wears a top hat.

showing the McLoughlins' world just as they left it when they died in the 1850s. Every detail was there—except for the McLoughlins themselves.

When the McLoughlins died, they were buried next to their beloved house. But in 1909 the house was moved to a nearby hilltop and restored to its past splendor. It took almost seventy more years before the graves of John and Marguerite followed the house to the hill. They must have liked the restoration, because it wasn't long before they moved back in.

The ghostly goings-on have scared many a worker away from the old museum. But director Nancy Wilson has had a twenty-year relationship with the ghosts and loves it. At first, Nancy and her workers heard only ghostly footsteps walking upstairs. It was nothing living, Nancy knew, but what was it?

Then she saw the shadow. One day, she entered the front door and glimpsed a tall, dark shape circle the stairway and dart into the dining room. Shortly after,

Those brave enough to walk by the McLoughlin House at night sometimes see phantoms in the second-floor windows.

Even before his death, John McLoughlin scared people with his wild hair and burning eyes.

she was coming down the stairs and heard something drop above her on the landing. She turned and caught the same shadow moving from the hall into John's bedroom. It was so tall it had to duck through the doorway.

It must be John McLoughlin, Nancy thought. John was a giant in his day—six feet, five inches tall with long, wild white hair. Surely he had to duck through doors. Then one day while vacuuming his room, she was tapped three times on the shoulder. Thinking it was a worker, she turned around, but no one was there. She was too scared to scream.

"I think the doctor likes women," Nancy says now. A disbelieving radio producer was doing a Halloween story a few years ago when she was pinched on the bottom by an unseen hand as she walked by John's room.

Does Marguerite know about her husband's flirting? Nancy's convinced she's there watching. Passing joggers have seen a woman at night standing in an upstairs window, and others have asked about the window mannequin in an old dress. There are no mannequins in the museum. One tourist thanked Nancy for having a woman dressed in nineteenth-century clothing in one of the rooms. Nancy just smiled and said, "We don't have one." The tourist turned white and left.

Ghost activities happen anytime. But the most predictable event happens once a year on the anniversary of John's death. Every September 3 at 9:35 A.M., when the sun hits his portrait downstairs over the fireplace, an eerie thing happens. Though the entire painting is sunlit, only his face begins to glow with a ghostly bright yellow light, as if John McLoughlin is ready to leap from the painting into life again.

White Eagle Tavern, Portland

HAUNTED BY
Rose and Joe

Chuck Hughes will never forget his first ghost encounter at the White Eagle. Soon after buying the one-hundred-year-old brick tavern in 1978, Chuck was tending bar on a hot summer night when a table of customers waved him over. Something was very wrong, they said. They could hear a woman crying, but they couldn't find her.

Chuck heard the sobbing too. He checked the bathrooms, the kitchen, and the basement but found nothing. Chuck figured it had to be coming from upstairs, but the only stairway was outside, and it was locked. Chuck left the bar, unlocked the stairway door, and climbed the dark passage. The second floor, which had once been a boardinghouse, had been sealed off since 1955. No one should have been in there.

The second floor of the White Eagle Tavern is so haunted that the owner won't let anyone enter—not even himself!

The long central hallway was dark. Chuck moved slowly, checking each bedroom for intruders. As he neared the end of the hall, he heard the crying coming from the darkness ahead. But he couldn't see, so he rushed back to the bar for a flashlight. He hurried back up the stairs and was halfway down the hall when he felt invisible hands grab his shoulders from behind. Chuck stopped dead in his tracks. The air turned stone cold and began to cover him like frozen arms. Terrified, Chuck hurried for the stairs, trying to brush off the ghostly cloak that covered him. Halfway down the stairs, the presence finally lifted, and Chuck looked up to see a smoky, shimmering form returning to the hallway. Chuck ran to his basement office, where he sat shaken and pale for the next two hours.

Even today, Chuck will not go upstairs at night; he respects the ghosts' privacy. After combing old records and accounts, Chuck believes the crying woman is Rose, who lived upstairs and was murdered by her boyfriend. The other ghost is Joe, a wandering worker who committed suicide in the boardinghouse. His clothes are still up there, and according to Chuck, they move from room to room.

Chuck met Joe in the basement after closing one night, a night he'd like to forget. Too tired to drive home, Chuck decided to sleep on a small bed near his desk. Just as he slipped into a deep sleep, his bed began bucking like a bronco. Chuck jumped to his feet, and the bed stopped. Confused and exhausted, he moved to his chair, propping his feet on the desk. As he drifted into sleep again, his feet were slapped off the desk along with his papers. Too terrified to sleep now, Chuck fled the bar and hasn't spent the night since. "They don't want me here all night," he says.

Sometimes when the bar is open, Chuck will see a terrified woman run from the bathroom, chased out by a blizzard of white paper. When he peeks into the ladies' room, Chuck sees toilet paper flying into the air from an empty stall. He can only shake his head and wonder what the next act will be from his dead entertainers.

The ghosts are so bold that they even show up inside the tavern, where they have been seen pouring themselves drinks, playing slot machines, and throwing toilet paper around the bathrooms.

WASHINGTON

E. R. Rogers Restaurant, Steilacoom

HAUNTED BY

The attic lady and a dining gentleman

Pike Place Market
Seattle
Harvard Exit Theater
Steilacoom
OLYMPIA ★ E. R. Rogers Restaurant
WASHINGTON

Enjoying a quiet drink in an elegant Victorian restaurant is normally not a terrifying experience. But it can be in the E. R. Rogers Restaurant. One night in 1982, shortly after Gordon

At the E. R. Rogers Restaurant, you never know who or what might join you for dinner.

Robertson bought the restaurant, a polite foreigner tipped back a beer in the second-floor bar after a long business day. As his head tilted and his eyes ran up the wall, he couldn't believe what he suddenly saw. Sitting on a thin, wooden ledge high above the bar was an old lady in stockings! When he jumped up to say something, she passed right through the wall, disappearing into the attic. The suddenly sober gentleman grabbed his hat and left.

No one knows for sure who the attic lady is. This one-hundred-year-old building has had many owners, but maybe it was just the perfect view over Puget Sound that attracted a lost soul. Whoever she is, she guards her attic well. The first time Gordon went up to the attic at night to get supplies, a board flew from nowhere and hit him in the head. The unfriendly greeting left its mark; he won't go up there at night anymore, and neither will his staff.

One night after Gordon had turned out the lights and locked up the restaurant, he looked back from his car and saw all the lights turn back on. Thinking there was a burglar, he called the police. A K-9 unit arrived, and the dog was sent in to scour the house. The dog searched the first two floors and found nothing. When he was ordered to search the attic, the dog refused. The officer went instead, leaving his four-legged partner behind. Though he found nothing, he could never explain his dog's terrible fear.

The attic lady shares the house with a gentleman ghost, whom waitresses see in the upstairs dining room—always sitting at the same table. He appears after closing, when the dining room is empty, wearing old clothes and eating an invisible dinner. In midmeal he fades away.

Gordon doesn't call the police anymore. He's learned to live with the lights going on and off at night, the bar TV changing channels by itself, the blender suddenly turning on, and the stereo turning off. He's lost workers to the ghosts—those who can't stand the feeling of being watched or followed. But mostly he gets a thrill out of his haunted restaurant. And once in a while, a lump on his head.

After seeing a ghostly old lady sitting on a ledge above the bar, one visitor ran from the restaurant too scared to even finish his beer.

Harvard Exit Theater, Seattle

HAUNTED BY

Women of the Century Club

If you leave your seat at the Harvard Exit Theater to use the bathroom, don't expect all the scary things to stay behind on the movie screen. One moviegoer had no reason to expect the gruesome scene that awaited her one evening in the third-floor ladies' room.

The staff remembers that night, in the mid 1990s, when a terrified woman came running from the third floor in tears. "There's a woman hanging in the  bathroom," she cried. The manager rushed upstairs and threw open the door. Just moments before, the petrified woman had seen a lady hanging from a rope suspended from the bathroom ceiling. When the manager looked, there was nothing, aside from the unusual chill that always filled this room.

Luckily for the theater, the usual ghost encounters are much less dramatic and nor-

The Harvard Exit Theater was Seattle's oldest women's club, and its long-dead members still gather in the lounge at night.

mally occur when the theater is closed for business. No one knows for sure whose spirits roam the movie house. In the early 1900s, the theater was a women's club with members from Seattle's most powerful families. The three-story brick build-ing had beautiful parlors and a grand playhouse. When a movie theater company bought it in 1970 and added a second the-ater on the third floor, some of the women's spirits were stirred into action.

The theater has a long elegant lobby filled with antiques, a pi-ano, and a fireplace. One day the manager came early to un-lock the lobby doors and start a fire. When she entered, she saw a woman dressed in Victorian clothing sitting in a chair in front of the fireplace. The sur-prised spirit looked up from a book she was reading, smiled, and slowly faded away. Other

If you've come to the theater to watch a movie, don't be surprised to feel the touch of an unseen hand.

times, the manager arrived to find a fire burning and chairs pulled around the hearth in a half-circle, as if a meeting had just ended.

None of the theater staff today likes going to the third-floor bathroom or the waiting lounge alone. Even the ones who don't know the hanging ghost story say they get chills there. Disembodied voices are heard coming from the lounge, and another woman in black has been spotted on the stairway to the third floor.

Although a few moviegoers have reported an invisible presence that plays with their hair in the upstairs theater, most of the ghosts seem to be active only after hours. The living have their time to laugh and cry at the ghosts of Hollywood. But when the theater closes, the real ones come out for another meeting of the phan-tom women's club.

Pike Place Market, Seattle

HAUNTED BY

An old Indian Woman and Little Boy

For years, the strangest shopper in Seattle's Pike Place Market was the ghost of an old Indian woman. The market has always been Seattle's center for selling and trading goods. Mysterious mazelike hallways wind through five stories of little shops. It was in these narrow passages that store owners first spotted the ancient native woman carrying woven baskets in and out of the crowded stores.

Seattle's ghost central is the Pike Place Market, where spirits and shoppers mingle in the maze of hallways and stores.

She seemed most at home in a small shop on the third level called the Craft Emporium. Owner Lynn Hancock remembers the day in 1982 when the Indian woman first entered her store and walked to the back to look at beads. When Lynn approached her, the old woman vanished into thin air. Lynn was so shaken that she asked the other customers to leave, and closed the store for the day.

The Indian woman became a regular visitor to the Craft Emporium, always looking at the same beads. Finally, Lynn hired a medicine man, who helped the old woman's spirit move to the next world. She hasn't been seen since.

However, all is not quiet at the Craft Emporium. As if a void were waiting to be filled, something else moved into the shop. Doreen Locati, the manager, noticed little things at first. When she opened the shop in the morning, she'd see beads lined up on the counter, on the floor, on the shelves, everywhere. Plumbing fixtures that ran along the ceiling would be unscrewed and placed neatly on the floor.

Soon, unexplainable things happened during business hours. Strands of beads would fly off shelves and cabinets, as if thrown. One customer watched in awe as tiny teddy bears, sitting quietly in a plastic tub, began jumping like popcorn onto the counter and floor. Recently, when a new employee put on her jacket to leave, beads came pouring from her sleeves.

Doreen suspected they might have a child ghost, given all the silly tricks. Then, one evening, she heard the voice of a little boy call her name. Last Halloween the same voice greeted the assistant manager with a "Happy Halloween" as she opened the store. They named the ghost Little Boy but have no idea who he is or why he has chosen to haunt the bead store. Sometimes he makes the puppets in the store next door dance by themselves, but usually he's happy in the Craft Emporium, as long as he can pull pranks on unsuspecting bead buyers.

The biggest joker is the littlest ghost—a young boy haunts the Craft Emporium and loves to rearrange the beads.

I N D E X